D1420895

9112000216477

BEHIND THE NEWS

HOSTAGE TAKERS

Philip Steele

WAYLAND

First published in 2014 by Wayland
Copyright © Wayland 2014

Wayland
338 Euston Road
London NW1 3BH

Wayland Australia
Level 17/207 Kent Street
Sydney, NSW 2000

All Rights Reserved.
Produced for Wayland by Tall Tree Ltd
Editors: Emma Marriott and Jon Richards
Designer: Malcolm Parchment

ISBN 978 0 7502 8254 3
E-book ISBN 978 0 7502 8816 3

Dewey number: 364.1'54-dc23

10 9 8 7 6 5 4 3 2 1

Printed in China

Wayland is a division of Hachette Children's
Books, an Hachette UK company
www.hachette.co.uk

The publisher would would like to thank the
following for their kind permission to reproduce
their photographs:

Shutterstock.com unless stated otherwise:
Front cover: ivstiv, bibikoff, bibiphoto
AFP/Getty Images (4), BortN66 (5), lynea (6),
© Bettmann/CORBIS (7), © STRINGER/INDIA/
Reuters/Corbis (8), Northfoto (9), Public domain
(10), © Jenny37 (11), BlueSkyImage (12),
Chris DeRidder (13), Getty Images (14),
David Fowler (15), © STRINGER/SOMALIA/Reuters/
Corbis (16), © Joseph Okanga/Reuters/Corbis (17),
Public domain (19), AFP/Getty Images (20),
Getty Images (21), Getty Images (22), Courtesy FBI
(23), Getty Images (25), Getty Images (25),
© GORAN TOMASEVIC/Reuters/Corbis (26), Getty
Images (27), © Reuters/CORBIS (28), © Reuters/
CORBIS (29), Public domain (30), Adam Gregor (31
- posed by model), © OSMAN ORSAL/Reuters/Corbis
(32), Public domain (33), © demotix/Demotix/Corbis
(34), Public domain (35),© Antonella865 (36),
Public domain (37), ChameleonsEye (38), © Derek
Gordon (39), © AGENCIA ESTADO/Xinhua Press/
Corbis (40), © AGENCIA ESTADO/Xinhua Press/
Corbis (41), ChameleonsEye (42), © Paul Fleet (43),
GMEVIPHOTO (44), © MOHAMED AZAKIR/Reuters/
Corbis (45)

CONTENTS

Held at gunpoint.....................4
The longer view.......................6
Acts of terrorism.....................8
Colombia, 2002–08.................10
Is it ever acceptable?..............12
Captivity................................14
Kenya and Somalia, 2011......16
Can all be forgiven?...............18
Negotiation............................20
Alabama, USA, 2013..............22
To pay or not to pay?............24
Risk and rescue.....................26

Moscow, Russia, 2002...........28
Are all lives equal?................30
Terror in the news.................32
Tigantourine, Algeria, 2013..34
Does the press help?.............36
Global justice........................38
Aracaju, Brazil, 2012.............40
Do the new laws work?.........42
Creating a safer world..........44
Glossary................................46
Index.....................................48

HELD AT GUNPOINT

Masked men seize a man on the street and bundle him into a car. A terrified woman stares from a video clip while her captors point guns at her. These are the images we see on front pages and screens every year, along with the words 'HOSTAGE CRISIS'.

What is hostage taking?

Hostage taking is a form of blackmail. The freedom, safety or life of a captive is threatened unless certain demands are met. The hostage takers may be asking for a ransom, political changes, the release of prisoners, or safe passage to another country. Sometimes hostages are held as 'human shields'. They are placed in a vulnerable location in order to deter an

Kidnappers will often release a video of the hostage in order to demean them or to force friends or governments to meet their demands.

attack by an enemy. When an aircraft, ship or vehicle is hijacked, the passengers held under threat are also called hostages.

How does it happen?

Hostage taking involves abduction, although in history abduction often happened as part of a diplomatic treaty or military exchange. Criminal abduction for profit is generally called kidnapping.

Investigating the problem

In this book we shall go behind the news headlines to find out more. Who are the hostage takers today, and what do they want? What drives them to extreme action? How does captivity and stress affect the victims? When should officials negotiate with hostage takers? How can lives be saved? How can we prevent hostage taking in the first place?

TERRORIST ATTACKS WORLDWIDE 2012

- **Number of terrorist attacks** 6,771
- **Number killed in terrorist attacks** 11,098
- **Number kidnapped or taken hostage** 1,283

'We were raped of our freedom, dignity and pride for 444 days.'

Rocky Sickmann, hostage during the Iran hostage crisis of 1979, *The Navy Times.*

THE LONGER VIEW

Hostage taking is often referred to as a problem of modern times but it has a history of at least 4,000 years. It has been practised not only by warriors, pirates, rebels and terrorists but also by regular armies, rulers and governments.

• Stories of hostage taking are found in the Bible and in ancient Greek myths and legends. The Egyptian and Hittite armies exchanged hostages in 1269 BCE.

• In Europe's Celtic Iron Age, children and adults were held hostage by some rulers as an insurance against rebellion or war. One High King of Ireland born in about 342 CE is known to history as Niall of the Nine Hostages. Keeping hostages could make a ruler powerful.

• In 1192, King Richard I of England was captured by Leopold V, Duke of Austria. Leopold demanded 6,000 buckets of silver coins as a ransom (worth about £2 billion today).

In 75 BCE, Julius Caesar was kidnapped and held hostage by Cilician pirates after they boarded his ship.

• Hostage taking is mentioned in the Magna Carta (Great Charter) signed by King John of England in 1215.

• Hostage taking was common practice in piracy and in wars from the 1600s to the 1800s. Governments, merchants and monks called 'Redemptionists' negotiated ransoms for Christian hostages held in the 'Barbary' (Berber) states of North Africa.

• During the American Civil War of 1861–65, both sides took hostages and used human-shield tactics. The taking and execution of hostages by Nazi troops was common in occupied Europe during World War II (1939–45).

• Terrorism and hostage taking were common policies of Middle Eastern states and of Jewish, Arab, Kurdish and Iranian militants between the 1940s and the present day.

• In 1972, the pro-Palestinian Black September group seized 11 Israeli athletes as hostages at the Olympic Games in Munich, Germany.

• Other trouble spots for hostage taking in the 1970s and 1980s included Central and South America, Europe and Asia. Political hostage taking by terrorist groups, such as the Provisional IRA in Northern Ireland and Italy's Red Brigades, became headline news.

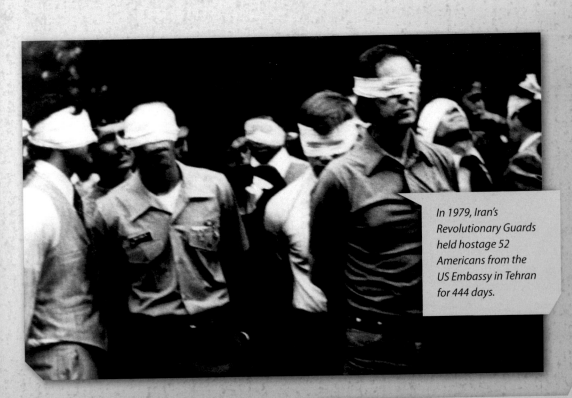

In 1979, Iran's Revolutionary Guards held hostage 52 Americans from the US Embassy in Tehran for 444 days.

ACTS OF TERRORISM

Modern hostage taking may have many motives. Very often it is part of a campaign of terrorism. Terrorism is a bid to bring about political or social change by striking fear into one's enemies or the general public.

Terrorist tactics

'Terrorism' was first used to describe the policy of a government – the French National Convention of 1793. Today, that type of rule is called state terrorism. 'Terrorists' are militant activists who use such tactics against governments.

Motives for menace

Terrorist hostage taking may take two forms. The first is sometimes described as 'instrumental'. It is a kind of leverage, designed to force a concession or a reward from the enemy. The second is 'expressive', meaning that its chief aim

Italian tour guide Paolo Bosusco, may have been taken hostage in 2012 by Indian Maoist rebels for instrumental reasons. Shortly after his release, the wife of one of his captors was released from prison.

is to demonstrate anger or revenge. It may be an act of propaganda, designed to intimidate the enemy or to impress one's own side. Other types of hostage taking might be unplanned or as a result of mental illness.

The victims

Hostages may be seized at random from the street. Some may belong to a group of people who are perceived as enemies, such as soldiers, or as helpers of the enemy, such as contractors. Civilians working in war zones are always vulnerable. Visitors to trouble spots, such as journalists, business people, political activists or missionaries, may also be at risk. Powerful politicians, wealthy bankers or senior army officers may bring the hostage takers the richest rewards.

People working in war zones, such as these Italian aid workers in Albania, are vulnerable to hostage taking.

WHERE ARE THE DANGER ZONES?

Abduction for ransom, January–July 2013
TOP COUNTRIES
1. Nigeria
2. Mexico
3. Pakistan
4. Yemen
5. Syria and Honduras
6. Colombia and India

1% Europe

19% Rest of Asia

36% Africa

17% Middle East

27% North and South America

COLOMBIA, 2002-08

In 2002, a presidential election campaign was underway in Colombia. Íngrid Betancourt Pulecio was standing for the Green Oxygen Party, which she had founded. She was an elected senator, and known for being an opponent of corruption.

Íngrid Betancourt was kidnapped when she was campaigning to become the country's president.

NEWS FLASH

Hostage: Íngrid Betancourt
Nationality: Colombian with dual French citizenship
Hostage takers: FARC (Revolutionary Armed Forces of Colombia)
Status: Guerrillas fighting the Colombian government since 1964. Listed as terrorist by the Colombian government, the USA and the EU, but recognised by some countries in South and Central America.
Demand: Hostages for prisoners exchange
Captivity: 6½ years
Resolution: Rescued by Colombian forces

Abduction by the rebels

Íngrid was canvassing in the region of San Vinente del Caguán where the FARC had a strong presence. On 23 February, her car was stopped at a rebel checkpoint and she and her aide, Clara Rojas, were abducted. This was not pre-planned, but rebels often took hostages in the hope of exchanging them for their own members held captive in Colombian jails.

A six-year ordeal

In 2003, the French Foreign Ministry attempted a rescue mission through Brazil.

However details of the mission were leaked and in the confusion, no contact was made with the FARC. Videos were released to prove that Íngrid was still alive. For more than six years, she and several other hostages were held at remote camps in the jungle, often caged or in chains. Íngrid became very thin and was in poor health. She endured beatings, insect bites and crushing boredom. She was determined to survive but there were tensions not only with her captors but also between her and some of her fellow hostages.

Rescue by helicopter

The international campaigners for Íngrid's release never gave up hope. At last, in 2008, the Colombian military announced that they had infiltrated the FARC forces and fooled them into allowing Íngrid and 14 other hostages to board a helicopter that was actually part of a rescue mission. On her release, Íngrid appealed for a regional diplomatic solution to the conflict. In 2012, the FARC agreed to end kidnapping for ransom. Peace talks were held again in 2013.

'In this condition of the most devastating humiliation, I still possessed the most precious of liberties, that no-one could take away from me: that of deciding who I wanted to be.'

Íngrid Betancourt, *Even Silence Has an End: My Six Years of Captivity in the Colombian Jungle*, 2010.

To try and prevent further kidnappings, the Colombian army protects tourist groups on expeditions into the country's forests.

IS IT EVER ACCEPTABLE?

It is said that 'one person's terrorist is another's freedom fighter'. Violent protest can certainly be used to achieve political freedom – many rebels have gone on to become respected leaders, such as Nelson Mandela, who served as president of South Africa.

Denying human values

Does it mean that acts such as hostage-taking are morally acceptable if the end result is beneficial – such as the overthrow of a repressive government? Surely all such acts demean the captive as an individual and as a human being, and demean the captor and the cause, too? A human being is more than just a commodity. Hostage taking is cruel and abusive. It has a devastating effect not just on the victims, but also on their families and friends. It may involve torture and result in death.

This shocking image is taken from a video released by the kidnappers of Italian aid worker Clementina Cantoni. She was held hostage in Afghanistan in 2005. She was eventually released unharmed after more than three weeks in captivity.

The state as terrorist

A trained soldier, like a hostage taker, is encouraged to think of the victim or enemy as an object, not as a person. Is there any moral difference between an army taking hostages and a group of terrorists who do the same thing? If a government orders the abduction of people, imprisons them without trial and uses them as bargaining counters, are its officials any more moral than hostage-taking terrorists?

'The terrible thing about terrorism is that ultimately it destroys those who practise it. Slowly but surely, as they try to extinguish life in others, the light within them dies.'

Terry Waite, English hostage held in Lebanon, 1987–91, *The Guardian*.

This protest in the USA aimed to draw attention to the detainment of prisoners at Guantanamo Bay Detention Camp. While the US government insists that those held there may be guilty of war crimes, others say they are hostages and are being held illegally.

DEBATE   Do hostage takers achieve their aims?

YES
Ransoms are often paid, prisoners are often released. Their cause becomes well known.

NO
Acts of terrorism always alienate popular support for a cause and only help its opponents.

CAPTIVITY

In 2013, hostages who were pinned down during a gun rampage in the Westgate shopping mall in Nairobi, Kenya, were numb with shock and disbelief. They faced terrible, life-threatening dilemmas. Should they run? Play dead? Hide, or fight back? How could they protect their children? Hostages who are seized and held for weeks, months or even years face an even greater ordeal.

This image shows the level of destruction caused by the four-day siege at the Westgate Mall in September 2013 in Nairobi, Kenya.

'Where am I?'

The first problem for abducted captives is disorientation. They may be blindfolded, hooded or gagged. Where are they being held? Does anyone know where they are? Is anyone going to rescue them? Who is holding them? They may be moved from one location to another, as the hostage takers try to avoid detection. They may be passed on from one group to another.

Brian Keenan was initially held hostage on his own, before sharing a cell with British journalist John McCarthy.

'It is a silent, screaming slide into the bowels of ultimate despair'

Brian Keenan, Irish hostage held in Lebanon, 1986–90.

An ongoing nightmare

The physical problems that captives face may vary, from discomfort to lack of food and water and sleep deprivation. The hostages may be missing vital medication. They could be chained or handcuffed for long periods of time and unable to exercise or move much. Captives are often starved, beaten, raped, interrogated and tortured, and are under the constant threat of being killed. Even if hostages are well treated, they are still being cruelly denied their freedom.

One day at a time

Hostages go through many raw emotions. They may be frozen in fear or full of rage. At times they may feel powerless. They may have moments of bravery, periods of resilience and hope, but they will also experience troughs of despair. One of the greatest difficulties is how to deal with the passing of time, how to keep the brain active and how to maintain one's identity and sense of self. The consoling fact is this: the longer the period of captivity, the greater the chance of survival.

KENYA AND SOMALIA, 2011

In the 2000s, Somalia was torn apart by fighting between Islamist factions, and by foreign attacks and invasions. There was a disastrous drought. Desperate fishermen turned to piracy and hostage taking. A militant Islamist faction called al-Shabaab kidnapped and murdered.

During her ordeal, Judith Tebbutt was insulted, humiliated and threatened with execution.

NEWS FLASH

Hostage: Judith Tebbutt
Nationality: British
Hostage takers: Somali pirates
Status: In 2011, the year of this abduction, around 3,000 to 5,000 Somali pirates were operating in the Indian Ocean. They made 151 attacks on ships that year, making a profit of about US$146 million. At the time this case was resolved in 2012, they were holding 159 hostages, mostly on ships.
Demand: Money
Captivity: 6 months
Resolution: Rescued after ransom of £600,000 was paid.

Holiday attack

In September 2011, an English couple named David and Judith Tebbutt booked a holiday to the Kenyan island of Kiwayu, near Lamu. David and Judith were staying in a remote tourist complex on the island. On the first night of their holiday, an armed gang attacked them in their tent. Judith was jabbed with the barrel of a rifle and dragged down to the beach where she was carried off to a waiting boat, which took her to the Somali coast. Only later did she find out that the captors had shot and killed her husband.

Held captive

Several days later, Judith found herself in Somalia, imprisoned in a small, windowless room. Her only food was a bowl of potatoes in the morning and rice in the evening. Judith took exercise and talked to her captors. Through her job as a social worker she had experience of dealing with difficult people in dangerous situations.

'I challenged them all through my captivity, and bossed them about a bit as well.'

Judith Tebbutt, *The Guardian.*

Ransom demand

Judith's captors used a satellite phone to speak with the outside world. When no money was forthcoming, the pirates threatened to shoot her. She was allowed to talk to her son Ollie, who was trying to arrange a deal. In February 2012, a private security firm secured Judith's release and she was flown back to Kenya. The British government has a policy of not paying ransoms, but some news reports suggested that one-third of the money came from its foreign aid budget.

One of the pirates, Ali Babitu Kololo, is escorted by police after being sentenced to death for his role in the kidnapping of Judith Tebbutt and the murder of David Tebbutt.

CAN ALL BE FORGIVEN?

Enduring a hostage crisis invites important questions about psychology. Relations between hostage takers and captors and also between fellow hostages may vary greatly over long periods.

DEBATE
Do hostages ever forgive captors for their crimes?

SOME DO
Four human rights activists from Christian Peacemaker Teams (CPT) were held hostage in Iraq by the Swords of Righteousness Brigade, from 2005 to 2006. One, Tom Fox, was killed. CPT declared, 'We forgive those who consider us their enemies.'

SOME DON'T
Politician Sigifredo López, held by the FARC in Colombia from 2002 to 2009, said he could never forgive his captors for the deaths of his 11 colleagues who were fellow hostages, killed during an attack.

How to survive

Preserving a sense of humanity and identity are key to survival. If the aim of the hostage takers is to dehumanise their captives, then the captives must establish with them a firm sense of identity and self-respect. Too much aggression towards the captor may result in an angry response. Too little may earn only contempt. The captive needs to understand the personalities of the guards and what is motivating them. It helps if the victim has knowledge of the culture and political or religious beliefs of the captors.

Common ground?

Are hostage takers open to an approach based on common humanity? Sometimes, but it does not alter the fact that the relationship cannot be an equal one – the hostage taker holds all the cards, the hostage has none.

In perhaps as many as one-quarter of crises, the hostage bonds with the captors. This has been called Stockholm syndrome, after a bank robbery hostage taking that occurred in Sweden in 1973. Does this help or hinder the situation? Probably the latter, say psychologists who liken such behaviour to domestic violence situations, where a victim cannot reject an abusive partner. It does not stop the abuse. In one incident, in 1974, US heiress Patty Hearst was abducted by a radical group known as the SLA (Symbionese Liberation Army). She joined them in their activities and even took part in a bank raid with them.

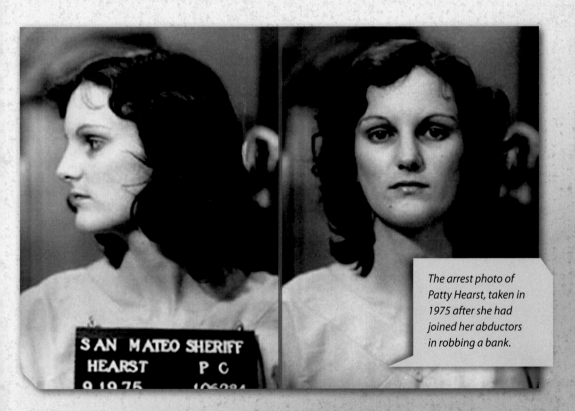

The arrest photo of Patty Hearst, taken in 1975 after she had joined her abductors in robbing a bank.

'What had I become? What had I descended to...
I walked the floor day after day, losing all
sense of the man I had been...'

Brian Keenan, *An Evil Cradling*, 1992.

NEGOTIATION

Hostages are virtually helpless when it comes to negotiations for their freedom. Even though these might be a matter of life and death, the outcome is not in their hands.

Crisis management

During a hostage situation, a specially trained law enforcement team may be called in to manage the event. The team will be advised by experts in the psychology of hostage taking. Their prime aim is to protect the lives of the hostages. The team tries to maintain contact with the hostage takers and defuse tension and anger and buy time. Concessions may be made to divert the captors from their chief demands.

Step-by-step

At the same time, the team needs to gather as much intelligence as it can, finding out about the situation on the ground and contacting anyone, such as

A Chinese man holds a woman hostage at knife point while a police negotiator (on the left) talks to him. The man later surrendered and released the hostage.

Hostage negotiator Terry Waite (far right) gives a press conference after negotiating the release of American hostages from Beirut in November 1986. Just months later Waite himself was taken captive and held for nearly five years.

friends and family, who might be able to persuade the hostage takers to surrender. Concessions to the hostage takers' demands may need discussions with others, such as national or foreign governments, or legal advisers. Negotiating may be part of a wider plan to enable intervention and rescue by a SWAT (Special Weapons and Tactics) team.

The longer road to release

Captors may release photographs or videos to prove that the hostages are still alive. Negotiations may take months or years and involve family members, friends, companies, governments and professional negotiators. Demands for conditions or money that are impossible to fulfil must be whittled down to an achievable deal.

'Freeing hostages is like putting up a stage set, which you do with the captors, agreeing on each piece as you slowly put it together; then you leave an exit through which both the captor and the captive can walk with sincerity and dignity.'

Terry Waite, former hostage in Lebanon, ABC television, 1986.

ALABAMA, USA, 2013

The big international hostage crises are often the ones that dominate the news, but incidents that involve fewer people can be every bit as terrifying – especially if the victim is a young child.

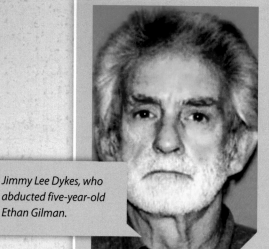

Jimmy Lee Dykes, who abducted five-year-old Ethan Gilman.

NEWS FLASH

Hostage: Five-year-old Ethan Gilman
Nationality: American
Hostage taker: Individual
Status: War veteran. International reports suggest that former soldiers often suffer from stress, breakdown in relationships, alcoholism, criminal and suicidal tendencies.
Demand: To broadcast a statement on television news.
Captivity: One week
Resolution: Rescued after hostage taker was shot dead

The bus attack

Disturbed and violent, 65-year-old Jimmy Lee Dykes was a veteran of the Vietnam War who mistrusted the US government. In January 2013, he boarded a school bus in Midland City, Alabama, and announced that he would take two boys hostage. A teenager called the emergency number 911 on his mobile phone. The bus driver, Charles Poland, blocked the aisle, allowing 21 children to escape from an emergency exit. Dykes fired a hand gun five times, shooting dead the driver, and then made off with five-year-old Ethan, who has Asperger's syndrome and ADHD.

In the bunker

Dykes took Ethan to an underground bunker that he had been preparing over the previous year. He then called 911 himself. Emergency services called in the FBI's Hostage Rescue Team (HRT). The HRT talked to Dykes through a ventilation pipe, and he demanded that a female reporter broadcast him live on the television news, after which he said he would commit suicide. He never revealed what his message to the world actually was. Dykes treated his hostage well and he agreed that medication and colouring books for Ethan could be passed down the pipe.

He even cooked him fried chicken. However, Dykes said that inside the bunker was a bomb that he was training Ethan to detonate. Ethan's mother asked the FBI not to harm Dykes if possible, as she believed he was mentally ill.

Assault and rescue

By the seventh day, negotiations were breaking down, and a spy camera revealed that Dykes was holding a gun. The FBI team used explosives to break into the bunker and tossed in stun grenades. They shot Dykes dead and Ethan was rescued successfully.

'He's my world. He's my everything. Everything I do, I do for him.'

Joyce Kirkland, Ethan's mother, CNN.

Dykes held Ethan Gilman hostage in this cramped underground bunker.

TO PAY OR NOT TO PAY?

Negotiating a ransom demand raises awkward ethical questions. Isn't the whole process a surrender to blackmail, which will encourage others to take hostages or prolong a conflict? Or does a threat to end a life override all theoretical considerations?

DEBATE

Should governments pay ransom demands?

YES

A government's first duty is to protect the lives and secure the freedom of its citizens.

NO

The payment of ransoms or other concessions to the captors only encourages more hostage taking. No payment, no deals – that is the best way to defeat the hostage takers in the long run.

'The payments of ransoms [are] beyond irresponsible. You can't even pretend you don't know where that money is going to: to purchase men and arms to use in violent conflict.'

Peter Pham, director of US-based research group Ansari Africa Center.

French president François Hollande welcomes hostages Marc Feret, Pierre Legrand, Daniel Larribe and Thierry Dol. The French intelligence agency denied suggestions that a ransom had been paid to secure their release in 2013 after three years in captivity in Niger.

Your money or your principles?

Perhaps the response should depend on the nature of the demand. Are some principles more readily sacrificed than others? How can someone place monetary value on any human life? Some governments announce in public that they do not pay ransoms, but then arrange for secret payments to be made, perhaps by other people. Is that hypocritical, or a sensible compromise?

Who has the final word?

Who should decide how negotiations proceed? One government may believe that an assault on the hostage takers' stronghold is necessary for political reasons, or another that no ransom should be paid on principle. Are they in a position to know best? If the friends and families of the hostages believe that is the wrong course of action, should the decision be theirs? Imagine what response you would want if it was your own father or your own sister who was bound to a chair with a sword or a pistol pointed at their head, or starving to death in a hut in the desert.

Debbie Calitz and Bruno Pelizzari return to South Africa to an emotional reception in 2012 after 20 months as hostages with Somali pirates.

RISK AND RESCUE

Many people believe that an assault on hostage takers should take place only if all other options have been exhausted, or if the killing of hostages seems imminent and preventable.

Going in...

Armed intervention poses a great risk to those held hostage. It requires acute judgment of the psychological state of the hostage takers or guards. Are they likely to be trigger-happy, desperate, weary or alert? Many other things also need to be considered, for example, is the building booby-trapped with explosives? The mental condition of the hostages must be taken into account, too. An attack could be a further and drastic shock for captives who are already traumatised or confused by their situation.

Police take cover outside the Westgate shopping mall in Nairobi, Kenya, where gunmen went on a shooting spree in 2013.

Deadly force

Untimely or rash intervention can have fatal consequences. It is not only the hostages and hostage takers whose lives are at risk. The assault team, emergency services, passers-by, or passengers in a hijacked vehicle may also be caught in a counter-attack or in the crossfire.

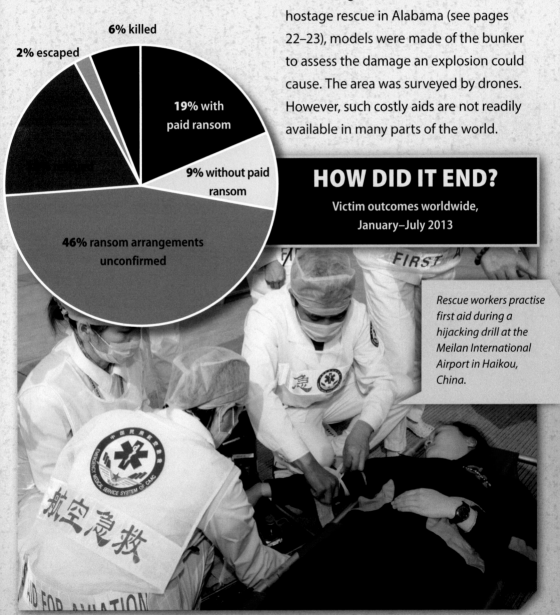

6% killed

2% escaped

19% with paid ransom

9% without paid ransom

46% ransom arrangements unconfirmed

HOW DID IT END?

Victim outcomes worldwide,
January–July 2013

It's all in the planning

Response teams must be highly trained, appropriately armed and ready for any eventuality. The operation must be carefully coordinated, with preparations made for the evacuation of survivors and wounded. The place of captivity must be studied in great detail. At the 2013 child hostage rescue in Alabama (see pages 22–23), models were made of the bunker to assess the damage an explosion could cause. The area was surveyed by drones. However, such costly aids are not readily available in many parts of the world.

Rescue workers practise first aid during a hijacking drill at the Meilan International Airport in Haikou, China.

MOSCOW, RUSSIA, 2002

On 23 October 2002, Moscow's Dubrovka Theatre was packed with an audience of more than 850 people. At about 9 pm, a bus drew up outside the theatre and 40 or more Chechen insurgents poured into the foyer, firing assault rifles in the air.

Movsar Barayev led the Chechen rebels during the theatre siege.

NEWS FLASH

Hostages: More than 850 theatre-goers
Nationality: Russians and foreigners
Hostage takers: Chechen separatists
Status: Insurgents have been demanding independence since the break-up of the old Soviet Union in 1990. There have been two wars in which the uprising has been brutally suppressed. After this hostage crisis, Russia stepped up the war and passed anti-terrorist legislation.
Demand: The withdrawal of Russian troops from Chechnya within one week
Captivity: Four days
Resolution: Attack by security forces

Besieged

Ninety or so theatre-goers made a quick escape and called the police. The Chechens released a further 150 to 200 people. Their main demand was that Russian troops withdraw from Chechnya within the week – an impossibly short timescale. A series of important public figures negotiated with the Chechens. The government offered the hostage takers safe passage to another country, but that was rejected.

Negotiations continued and further hostages were released, but the Chechens repeated their threat to kill if their demands were not met.

Gas and guns

Meanwhile the surrounding buildings, streets and even the sewers beneath the theatre were occupied by the security forces. Some people who tried to enter the theatre were shot dead by the rebels.

On the morning of 26 October, special forces stormed the theatre. Two hostages were killed by the Chechens. The Russians began to pump an unknown gas into the theatre, causing panic. A gun battle followed. The Chechens were all killed. Few ambulances were on hand, just buses. No details of the gas were released and 73 hostages received no treatment at all for its effects. In all, about 130 hostages died, mostly from the effects of the gassing.

Grainy images show Russian special forces carrying unconscious hostages from the Dubrovka Theatre after the attack.

'The operation was carried out brilliantly by special forces.'

Yuri Luzhkov, Mayor of Moscow.

ARE ALL LIVES EQUAL?

A hostage crisis raises many dilemmas. What costs and what risks are acceptable? Should the lives of many be put in danger to save a few? Such questions cannot really be answered except by the rescue teams and emergency services who risk their lives.

DEBATE

Should the hostage takers lives be spared?

YES

If the hostages can be rescued, the hostage takers' lives should also be spared. They should stand trial for their crimes. Terrorism can be defeated only by the rule of law.

NO

The priority has to be to prevent the hostage takers killing others. If that means that they die, then that is the risk they have brought upon themselves through their actions.

Three US marines rehearse a hostage rescue situation during an exercise.

The aftermath

The 'outcome' or 'resolution' of a hostage crisis is generally defined in terms of fatalities or ransom payments and rescue. For those fortunate enough to survive, the outcome really lies in the years that follow. Former hostages may suffer from post-traumatic stress, reliving the horrors they have been through. Child hostages especially may have been damaged by the experience. Victims may be overwhelmed by grief or by feelings of guilt if fellow hostages did not survive the ordeal.

Picking up the pieces

It may be hard for victims to reconnect with the real word. Relationships or marriages may break up, even when the partner has spent years campaigning for the release of the hostage, because the person who emerges from a long captivity is different from the person the partner knew before. It may be very difficult for people to return to work. If a rescue team brings one chapter of the hostage's story to a close, a counsellor or psychiatrist may be needed to help begin the next one.

Many former hostages need a long period of counselling in order to come to terms with the ordeal they have been put through.

'Freedom comes slowly at first.'

Brian Keenan, *An Evil Cradling*, 1992.

TERROR IN THE NEWS

Hostage takers and the media have a close and often unhealthy relationship. The media feed off terrorism because heartbreaking, gruesome stories sell newspapers and get ratings. In turn, terrorists thrive on the publicity and the spreading of fear.

Media messages

Hostage takers may use the press as a way of keeping up the pressure in their bid for a ransom or a political concession. A video clip may be slipped to the press showing harrowing scenes of captives being forced to read out a statement or making a desperate plea for their lives. Even more horrific are cases where the execution of a hostage is shown, to prove that the threat to murder other hostages is real. At any critical point in a hostage crisis, official negotiators may call for a 'media blackout', so that press reports do not upset delicate negotiations or place the hostages at risk or distress their families.

The Turkish government successfully negotiated the release of two pilots in 2013, including Murat Akpinar shown here, in return for the release of nine Lebanese hostages by rebels in Syria.

French reporters Hervé Ghesquière and Stéphane Taponier were held hostage by the Taliban for 18 months before being released in 2011. The Taliban claimed they were freed in exchange for the release of several imprisoned Taliban fighters.

DEPUIS 500 JOURS, HERVÉ ET STÉPHANE SONT OTAGES EN AFGHANISTAN.

REPORTERS SANS FRONTIÈRES

Reporting or distorting?

Reporters themselves are often victims of hostage taking, partly because they visit war zones and trouble spots and partly because they have a high public profile. Journalists have a duty to report news accurately and fairly, to look at the reasons for conflict and to examine cruelty or lawlessness. However, some press coverage of hostage crises is sensationalist, lurid and inaccurate. This may stoke up public anger, fear and misunderstanding, creating the very atmosphere in which terrorism thrives.

'... while you have to be competent to pull off a terrorist attack, you don't have to be competent to cause terror. All you need to do is start plotting an attack and — regardless of whether or not you have a viable plan, weapons or even the faintest clue — the media will aid you in terrorizing the entire population.'

Bruce Schneier, US writer.

TIGANTOURINE, ALGERIA, 2013

Tigantourine is a natural gas production site located near the town of In Amenas. In 2013, the labour force, chiefly Algerian, also included expatriate workers from around the world. These were troubled times in neighbouring countries Libya and Mali.

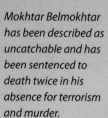

Mokhtar Belmokhtar has been described as uncatchable and has been sentenced to death twice in his absence for terrorism and murder.

NEWS FLASH

Hostages: More than 800 workers
Nationality: 668 Algerians, 132 foreign nationals
Hostage takers: The Masked Brigade, linked to al-Qaeda
Status: An Islamist group founded by Algerian Mokhtar Belmokhtar. Belmokhtar funded his campaigns by kidnapping and was said to be able to get US$3 million for a European captive.
Demands: An end to French military intervention in Mali, release of prisoners
Captivity: Four days
Resolution: Attack, 67 casualties

Terrorist bombs

At 5:45 am on 16 January, about 40 terrorists attacked buses taking workers to Tigantourine from a housing compound. The terrorists belonged to an al-Qaeda faction recently formed by veteran hostage taker Mokhtar Belmokhtar, an Algerian. Some of the victims were killed and others taken hostage. The terrorists then entered the buildings at the site and rigged up explosives. They hunted for foreign workers. Altogether, 800 people were seized as hostages, of whom 132 were foreigners.

Some hostages were gagged, bound or beaten. Others were shot in the head, some were wired with explosives and several escaped.

Airborne response

The hostage takers were calling for an end to French attacks on militants in northern Mali. The Algerian government declared that it did not make deals with terrorists, and surrounded the site with troops. The hostage takers' commander, Abu al-Baraa, phoned the Aljazeera television news channel and demanded the withdrawal of the troops and a release of prisoners.

On the afternoon of 17 January, Algerian special forces launched an assault on the site with helicopter gunships. The attack lasted 8 hours and at least 67 people were killed, of whom 29 were hostage takers.

Media coverage

This hostage taking was the most important news story of the week around the world. As shocked and exhausted survivors came to terms with their ordeal, news broadcasts and reports analysed the tragedy and the rescue policy of the Algerian government, which had cost so many lives.

Algerian forces used helicopter gunships, such as this Mi-24, as part of the attack on the hostage takers.

'Foreign workers such as employees at BP's In Amenas facilities would be at risk especially while travelling by road.'

An unheeded warning from risk assessors Exclusive Analysis, issued months before the 2013 attack, CNBC.

DOES THE PRESS HELP?

Hostage and prisoner-of-war plots inspire many television thrillers, such as the US television series *Homeland* (2011–). A fictitious plot is one thing, but can an interest in real-life hostage crises be regarded as ghoulish?

RADIO TELEVISION DIGITAL NEWS ASSOCIATION

The Association of Electronic Journalists, Canada
CODE OF ETHICS
Article 10
Reporting on criminal activities such as hostage takings, prison uprisings or terrorist acts will be done in a fashion that does not knowingly endanger lives, offer comfort and support or provide vital information to the perpetrator(s). RTDNA members will contact neither victims nor perpetrators of a criminal activity during the course of the event for the purpose of conducting an interview that would interfere with a peaceful resolution.

Press ethics

Journalists may have a duty to inform the public of atrocities and public danger, but surely they also have a duty to uphold human dignity and not to intrude on the grief of relatives? Is it right for cameras to record images of the dead and dying after an attack on or by hostage takers? Should people be banned from using social media, such as YouTube, to show video clips of such scenes? Or does such a ban amount to censorship?

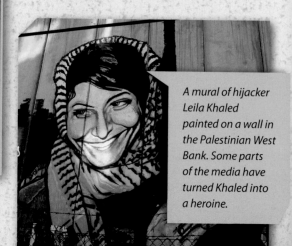

A mural of hijacker Leila Khaled painted on a wall in the Palestinian West Bank. Some parts of the media have turned Khaled into a heroine.

How it really is

Journalists sometimes portray the hostage takers as comic-strip stereotypes – the 'mad and evil genius', the 'beautiful but deadly female'. These images distort reality and may end up helping terrorists by giving them notoriety. Responsible reporting needs to be factual and calm. Journalists need to investigate the motives of the hostage taker, the precautions taken, the management of the crisis and the lessons learned. Unless fact is kept separate from fiction, hostage taking will not be understood or prevented.

In Manila, 2010, hostages were held captive in a bus. The failed rescue attempt and gun battle was watched by millions on the TV and internet.

DEBATE

Is a media blackout during a hostage crisis always a good idea?

YES

It can save lives. Irresponsible reporting of a hostage taking on a bus in the Philippines in 2010 made a bad situation much worse, with nine fatalities in a shoot-out.

NO

Lack of up-to-date information can hamper a public campaign for the release of hostages and only create false rumours and confusion.

GLOBAL JUSTICE

Criminal justice systems around the world define the illegality of kidnapping, abduction and hostage taking and set the punishments for those found guilty.

Enforcing the law

In practice, justice is often hard to achieve. Many hostage takers are already prepared to die or commit suicide before they act, so punishment for breaking laws, however harsh, may not act as a deterrent. Perpetrators may not be captured, but killed during a rescue bid. Hostage taking often takes place in regions such as war zones or disputed territory, where the rule of law is hard to enforce. Hostage taking is often a trans-national operation, crossing borders and involving many different nationalities. Extradition and international agreements may complicate the legal process. Laws may be waived as part of a deal, with hijackers or terrorists being allowed safe passage to another country.

Israeli soldiers capture a 'terrorist' during an urban warfare training exercise.

HOSTAGE TAKING AND INTERNATIONAL LAW

- 1625: Dutch legal expert Hugo Grotius writes about the ethics of hostage taking in *On the Law of War and Peace.*
- 1948: Trials held at Nuremberg in Germany, following World War II, confirm that hostage taking is allowed in war as a matter of last resort.
- 1948: Articles of the United Nations Declaration of Human Rights are incompatible with hostage taking.
- 1949: The Geneva Convention places an outright ban on hostage taking.
- 1979: A United Nations treaty, now known as the Hostages Convention, obliges participating nations to prosecute or extradite hostage takers.

Prevention and training

Prevention is generally the most effective policy. At government level, this may include increasing security at airports or gathering intelligence. In recent years, international naval patrols in the Indian Ocean have been effective in reducing hostage taking by Somali pirates. At a private level, many companies and organisations have also stepped up security and trained their staff in ways to avoid or survive a hostage crisis.

An Amphibious Assault Ship cruises the waters of the Persian Gulf. Such a show of strength can be used to prevent hostage-taking or to force another government to negotiate the release of hostages.

'Wherever law ends, tyranny begins.'

John Locke, *Two Treatises of Government*, 1689.

ARACAJU, BRAZIL, 2012

In a jail, all the power lies with the prison authorities. In order to make demands, prisoners may resort to riots or hostage-taking. In Brazil poor, overcrowded prison conditions are common grievances. In 2012, the strict regime at the 'Compajaf' caused anger and frustration to boil over.

Prisoners riot at the Compajaf Penitentiary Complex in Brazil.

NEWS FLASH

Hostages: 131 visitors and prison guards
Nationality: Brazilian
Location: Aracaju, northeastern Brazil
Hostage takers: Rioters in the Advogado Antonio Jacinto Filho Penitentiary Complex (known in short as the 'Compajaf')
Status: Prisoners
Demands: Change in jail management and better conditions.
Captivity: 26 hours
Resolution: Hostages released

Held hostage by rioters

A riot broke out in the Compajaf on 15 April 2012. Some 470 prisoners were demanding the dismissal of the governor. They also wanted better living conditions, no more abuse by the guards and an end to humiliating searches of female visitors.

Mattresses were set on fire and rebels climbed onto the roof, masking their faces from the press cameras below. Three rifles were seized from the gun room while other rebels armed themselves with knives. Three guards were taken hostage along with 128 visitors to the prison.

Release

A force of 150 police was sent in to restore order in the prison. Officials cut off the prison's supply of electricity and it was restored only after the hostage takers released 28 hostages. Negotiations went on for a day but to no avail. The authorities said that they were powerless to change the prison management without a court order, but they agreed to investigate the other complaints made by the hostage takers. The prisoners then released the hostages unharmed. The five ringleaders were transferred to another prison. The hostage takers had succeeded in one thing – placing the dire conditions in Brazilian jails under the spotlight of the international media.

Riot police were called in to restore order inside the prison, but the hostages were released after negotiations with the prisoners.

'I want perpetual imprisonment in Brazil for serious crimes against life, like those committed with premeditation and with cruelty. But I also want the same society that demands this to have legitimacy to apply such change. And this means basic conditions in prisons. With prisons ...which shame[s] us before Brazil and the world, our legitimacy becomes compromised.'

Diego Casagrande, journalist, *Metro Jornal*.

DO THE NEW LAWS WORK?

Following the Moscow theatre hostage crisis of 2002 (see pages 28–29), the Russian parliament approved new anti-terrorism laws. In the 2000s, many European countries also revised their laws on detention, making it easier for governments to combat terrorism.

Law and liberty?

Such laws were welcomed by most politicians and by many members of the public. They were criticised by others, who feared that basic civil liberties were being sacrificed. Were these governments still able to claim the high moral ground? Is not the maintenance of essential freedoms the best and most public way to reject the inhuman tactics of the hostage takers?

> ## Those who 'can give up essential liberty to obtain a little temporary safety deserve neither liberty nor safety.'
>
> Benjamin Franklin, *Historical Review of Pennsylvania*, 1759.

Some believe that security surveillance, such as this from Ashkelon, Israel, is an invasion of privacy and an attack on people's rights.

The use of unmanned drone aircraft to attack insurgents has only increased public anger in many parts of the world.

Is might the right response?

Similar issues arise if a government orders military action to prevent or punish a hostage crisis. Surely, many argue, it is best to destroy militants' bases so that they cannot strike again? And is this not just repaying the terrorists in kind, using the language that they understand?

Yemen has suffered horrific losses in recent years from terrorist attacks and hostage taking. The US response has been to target the militants with remotely operated armed drones. However, in 2013 the Human Rights Watch organisation reported that in 6 cases it had studied, 57 of the 82 people killed were innocent civilians. Such attacks are said to be creating a wave of public anger in Yemen. Instead of preventing future hostage crises, might they be doing just the opposite?

DEBATE

Are powerful anti-terrorism laws necessary to stop the hostage takers?

YES

In times of crisis the strongest measures possible must be brought in to protect the public.

NO

If we throw away our hard-won freedoms, we are doing the terrorists' job for them.

CREATING A SAFER WORLD

Every individual case of hostage taking has different dimensions, so various practical solutions may apply. Prevention, training, armed response, negotiating methods, psychology, law and media issues may all play key roles in ending this terrible practice.

The roots of the problem

The real roots of hostage taking and other tactics of terror run deep and are difficult to tackle. Violence, crime and religious or political fanaticism do not spring from nowhere. They are bred in conditions of poverty, injustice, powerlessness and despair, where people's voices go unheard. They may be a response to oppression or state terrorism. Unchecked mental health problems may also drive people to commit acts of desperation and violence. Only if these problems are addressed, will the world become safer.

Anti-government protestors take to the streets in Venezuela. When protest is shut down, the likelihood of terrorist incidents such as hostage taking increase. A safer world is one in which genuine democracy and human rights are respected.

The release of a hostage is an emotional time, as these Lebanese hostages freed in 2012 found out on return to Beirut.

Precious freedom

News headlines of hostage crises may shock and horrify viewers and readers but these events are mercifully rare. Although they must be prepared for, they should not dominate the way people live their lives or be allowed to compromise people's freedoms, otherwise everyone becomes hostages. The best response to terrorism is to refuse to be terrorised and to carry on living life normally, from day to day.

[It is] 'imperative that we take steps to ensure that kidnap for ransom is no longer perceived as a lucrative business model and that we eliminate it as a source of terrorist financing.'

Mark Lyall Grant, Britain's ambassador to the UN, 2014.

GLOSSARY

abduction
Taking someone away or carrying them off, secretly or by force.

ADHD
Short for Attention Deficit Hyperactivity Disorder. Various types of behaviour that demonstrate a short span of attention, distraction, restlessness, talking too much or taking action without thinking it through.

al-Qaeda
Meaning 'the Base' in Arabic, this is a group of militant Islamists who have carried out major terrorist attacks in various parts of the world, including the 9/11 attacks on New York City, or trained others to do so. Their leadership included the Saudi Arabian Osama bin Laden (1957–2011).

Asperger's syndrome
A condition where a person has difficulties with social interaction and non-verbal communication and shows symptoms that are related to forms of autism.

blackmail
Demanding payment or other reward by intimidation and threats.

casualty
Someone who is killed or wounded.

Cilician
Someone who came from ancient Cilicia, a region that is now part of southern Turkey.

concession
An act or condition that is given away or yielded during negotiations.

drone
Also known as an 'unmanned aerial vehicle' or UAV, this is a remotely piloted aircraft, which may be used for surveillance, exploration or military attack.

expatriate
Someone living or working in a country other than his or her own.

extradition
Using international law to bring someone from one country to another to face justice.

fatality
A death.

foreign national
Someone holding the citizenship of another country.

guerrilla

An irregular fighter who attacks the enemy with surprise raids or ambushes rather than facing an opponent in open battle.

hijack

To seize a car, bus, truck, boat or plane by force.

hostage crisis

A stand-off between the authorities and hostage takers.

illegality

Contravention of the law.

insurgent

Someone who takes part in an armed uprising.

media blackout

When media organisations do not refer to an event in news broadcasts or reports, for security reasons.

moral

Describing something that is right, as opposed to something that is wrong, which is called immoral.

negotiate

To try to agree a deal by discussion.

notoriety

Being famous for all the wrong reasons.

post-traumatic stress

Anxiety and distress caused by reliving a horrific or violent experience, such as being held hostage or experiencing a terrorist act or warfare.

ransom

A sum of money paid to secure the release of a hostage or prisoner.

rebel

A person who refuses to obey orders, or opposes those in authority.

Redemptionists

Christian monks belonging to an order that negotiated ransoms for Christians who were held captive in North Africa in the 1600s.

state terrorism

Acts of political intimidation carried out by a government.

stereotyping

The portrayal of individuals as a standardised type.

Stockholm syndrome

A psychological state in which hostages or captives feel sympathy towards their captors and may even join in with their activities.

terrorism

Acts of violence intended to strike fear into the public or one's opponents for a political end.

veteran

An experienced or former soldier.

INDEX

A

aid workers 9, 12
Akpinar, Murat 32
Aljazeera 35
al-Qaeda 34
armed intervention 26, 27

B

Barayev, Movsar 28
Barbary states 7
Belmokhtar, Mokhtar 34
Betancourt, Ingrid 10, 11
Black September group 7
blackmail 4
Bosusco, Paolo 8

C

Calitz, Debbie 25
Cantoni, Clementina 12
Casagrande, Diego 41
Chechen separatists 28, 29
Civil War, American 7
Compajaf 40, 41
counselling 31

D

Dol, Thierry 25
drones 27, 43
Dykes, Jimmy Lee 22, 23

E

expressive hostage taking 8

F

FARC 10, 11, 18
FBI 23
Feret, Marc 25
Franklin, Benjamin 42

G

Ghesquière, Hervé 33
Gilman, Ethan 22, 23
governments 4, 6, 7, 8, 13, 17, 24
Grant, Mark Lyell 45
Guantanamo Bay Detention Camp 13

H

Hearst, Patty 19
Holland, François 25
Human Rights Watch 43
human shields 4

I

instrumental hostage taking 8
international law 39
Iran hostage crisis 5, 7

J

John, King 7
Julius Caesar 6

K

Keenan, Brian 15, 19, 31
Khaled, Leila 36
kidnapping 5
Kirkland, Joyce 23
Kololo, Ali Babitu 17

L

Larribe, Daniel 25
Leopold V, Duke of Austria 6
Legrand, Pierre 25
Locke, John 39
Luzhkov, Yuri 29

M

Magna Carta 7
Mandela, Nelson 12
Masked Brigade 34
McCarthy, John 15
media 32, 33, 36, 37
code of ethics 36
mental illness 9, 22, 23
Moscow theatre seige 28, 29, 42

N

negotiating 20, 21, 24, 25, 41
Niall of the Nine Hostages 6

P

Pham, Peter 24
Pelizzari, Bruno 25
pirates 6, 16, 25, 39
Poland, Charles 22
prisoners 40, 41
protest, violent 12
Provisional IRA 7
psychiatrists 31

R

ransom 4, 6, 7, 9, 11, 13, 16, 17, 24, 25, 27, 45
Red Brigades 7
Redemptionists 7
Richard I, King 6
riot police 41

S

Schneier, Bruce 33
special forces 21, 29, 30, 35
Stockholm syndrome 19

surveillance 42
Swords of Righteousness Brigade 18
Symbionese LIberation Army 19

T

Taliban 33
Taponier, Stéphane 33
Tebbutt, Judith 16, 17
terrorists 6, 8, 9, 38, 43

V

videos 4, 21, 32, 36

W

Waite, Terry 13, 21
Westgate shopping mall 14, 26
World War II 7

BEHIND THE NEWS

978-0-7502-8252-9

978-0-7502-8255-0

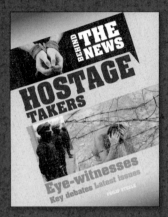

978-0-7502-8254-3

978-0-7502-8256-7

978-0-7502-8253-6

978-0-7502-8257-4

WAYLAND